Microsoft Word 2013 Expert

Michelle N. Halsey

ISBN-10: 1-64004-159-1

ISBN-13: 978-1-64004-159-2

Silver City Publications & Training, L.L.C.
P.O. Box 1914
Nampa, ID 83653
https://www.silvercitypublications.com/shop/

Contents

Chapter 1 – Customizing Word

In this chapter, you'll understand how to control the environment where you create documents, as well as specialized information about those documents. We'll start with customizing your Word options to make the environment perfectly suited to your use. Then, you'll learn how to protect a document. You'll also learn how to check for issues when working with others who are using earlier versions of Word. This module also explains how to manage different versions of a document. Finally, you'll learn the basics of the document properties and information.

Setting Word Options

To review the options for customizing Word, use the following procedure.

Step 1: Select the **File** tab from the Ribbon to open the Backstage view.

Step 2: Select the **Options** tab on the left.

Here is the General tab in the Word Options dialog box. The General tab allows you to change the user interface options. You can enter your name and initials to personalize your copy of Word. You can also control Start up options.

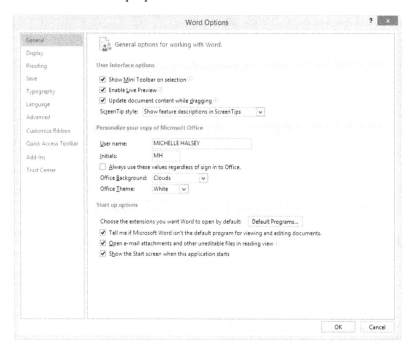

Here is the Display tab in the Word Options dialog box. The Display tab controls the Page display, the formatting marks, and the printing options.

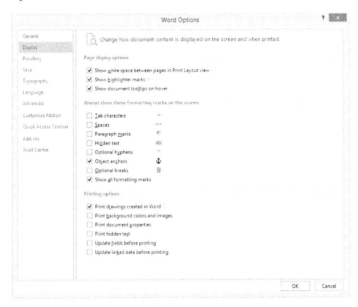

Here is the Proofing tab in the Word Options dialog box. The Proofing tab allows you to control how Autocorrect works for spelling, grammar, and formatting.

Here is the Save tab in the Word Options dialog box. The Save tab allows you to control how documents are saved.

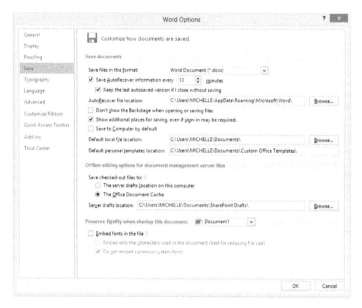

Here is the Typography tab in the Word Options dialog box. The Typography tab allows you to control character sets, character spacing, and kerning.

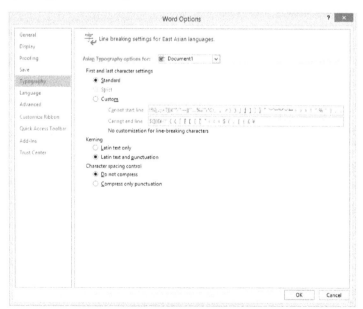

Here is the Language tab in the Word Options dialog box. The Language tab allows you to choose a language for use while editing your documents, which controls the spell checker and grammar. You can also change the language of the help files.

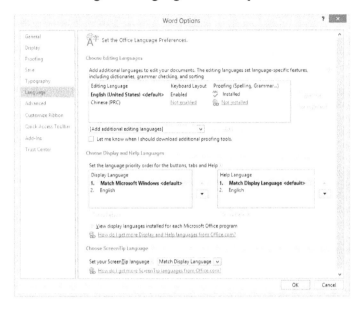

Here is the Advanced tab in the Word Options dialog box. In the Advanced tab, you can change a number of editing options, including the default paste option.

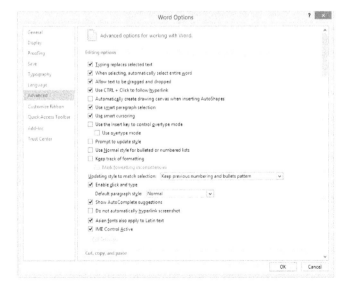

Protecting a Document

Use the following procedure to password protect a document.

Step 1: Select the **File** tab from the Ribbon to open the Backstage view.

Step 2: Select **Info**, if it isn't already selected.

Step 3: Select **Protect Document**.

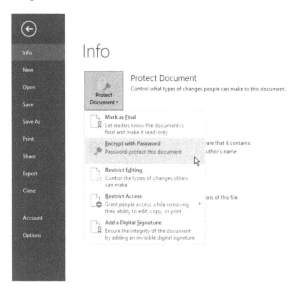

Step 4: Select **Encrypt with Password**.

Step 5: Enter a password and select OK. Make sure to keep the password safe, because the file cannot be recovered if you lose the password.

Checking for Issues

To inspect a document for hidden properties or personal information, use the following procedure.

Step 1: Select the **File** tab from the Ribbon to open the Backstage view.

Step 2: Select **Info**, if it isn't already selected.

Step 3: Select **Check for Issues**.

Step 4: Select **Inspect Document**.

Step 5: In the Document Inspector dialog box, check the box(es) for the types of issues you want to check for.

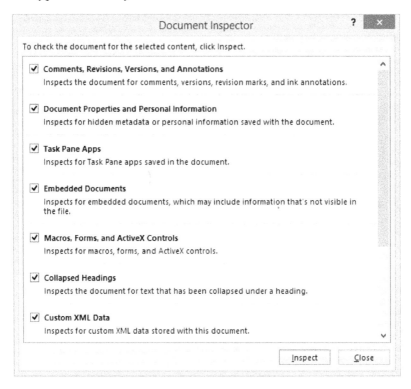

Step 6: Select **Inspect**.

Step 7: The Document Inspector dialog box indicates any issues with the document. You can select **Remove All** to remove the features from the document.

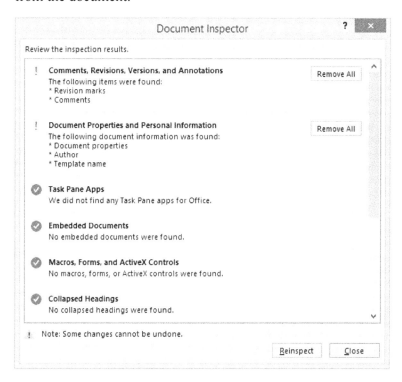

To review the Accessibility Checker, use the following procedure.

Step 1: Select the **File** tab from the Ribbon to open the Backstage view.

Step 2: Select **Info**, if it isn't already selected.

Step 3: Select **Check Accessibility**.

The Accessibility Checker appears on the right side of the document window. The Inspection Results area highlights any problems. You can click on an item in the list to go to that item to correct it. You can also why to fix and how to fix the item.

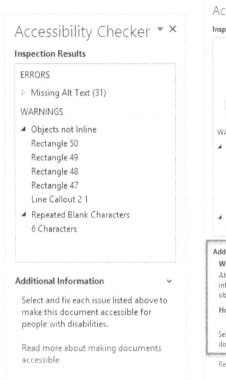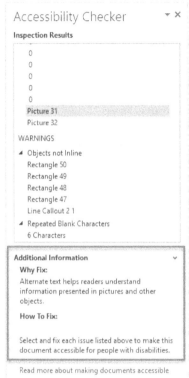

Use the following procedure to review the Compatibility Checker.

Step 1: Select the **File** tab from the Ribbon to open the Backstage view.

Step 2: Select **Info**, if it isn't already selected.

Step 3: Select **Check Compatibility**.

The Microsoft Word Compatibility checker dialog box shows features that are not supported by earlier versions of Word. You can select the version of Word from the **Select Versions to Show** drop down list.

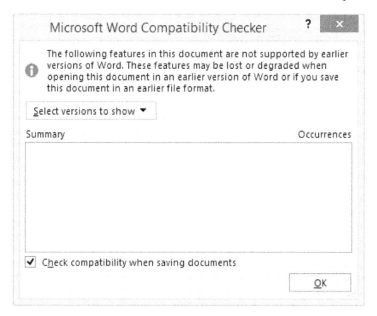

Managing Versions

To use the Manage Versions feature, use the following procedure.

Step 1: Select the **File** tab from the Ribbon to open the Backstage view.

Step 2: Select **Info**, if it isn't already selected.

Step 3: The Versions area includes the most recent versions of the document. You can select one to return to it.

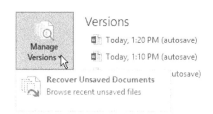

Step 4: Or, select **Manage Versions**.

Step 5: Select **Recover Unsaved Documents**.

Step 6: The Open dialog box displays a list of your unsaved files. Highlight the file and select Open.

Step 7: Make sure you save the file.

Working with Properties

To review the information contained in the Information tab on the Backstage View, use the following procedure.

Step 1: Select the **File** tab on the Ribbon to open the Backstage View.

Step 2: It should open to the **Info** tab. If not, select it from the left side of the screen.

Discuss the different information included in the Properties area.

Step 3: Select the **Show All Properties** link at the bottom to see additional information.

Step 4: You can chance the Title, Tags, Status, Categories, Subject, Hyperlink Base, and Company information.

To view or add People information, use the following procedure.

Step 1: To view an author or last modified person, click on the name. You can see the Microsoft Office contact card for that person.

Step 2: To add an author or manager, click on the Specify the Manage or Add an Author field. Enter the name. You can use the icons to verify the information or use the Address book to find the name.

To open the Advanced Properties dialog box, use the following procedure.

Step 1: Select the arrow next to **Properties**.

Step 2: Select **Advanced Properties** from the drop down list.

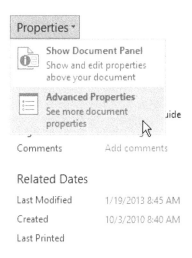

Discuss the tabs in the Advanced Properties dialog box.

The General tab includes information about the type, location, and size of the document file. You can also see when the document was created, modified, and accessed.

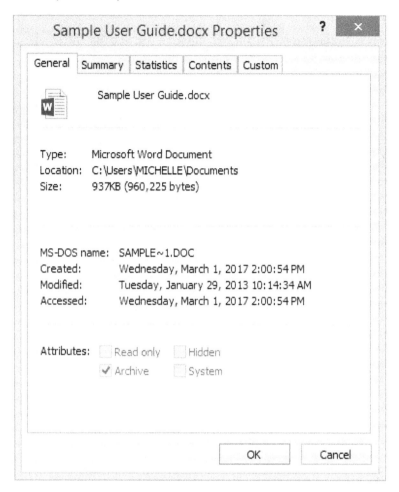

The Summary tab includes details about the document title, subject, author, etc. You can enter information in any of the Summary fields.

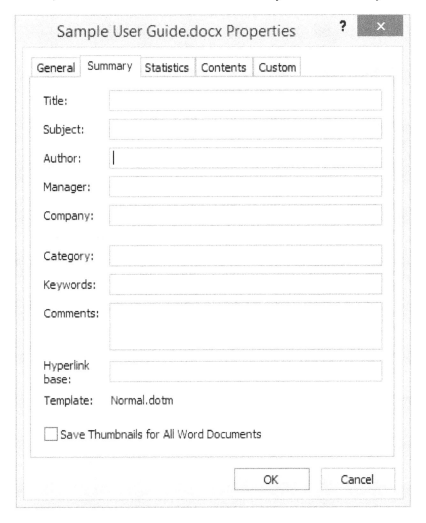

The Statistics tab includes information about the document revisions and other statistics.

Sample User Guide.docx Properties

General | Summary | Statistics | Contents | Custom

Created: Monday, September 27, 2010 8:34:00 AM
Modified: Tuesday, January 29, 2013 10:14:34 AM
Accessed: Wednesday, March 1, 2017 2:00:54 PM
Printed:

Last saved by:
Revision number: 12
Total editing time: 38 Minutes

Statistics:

Statistic name	Value
Pages:	11
Paragraphs:	47
Lines:	105
Words:	891
Characters:	4029
Characters (with spaces):	4887

OK | Cancel

The Contents tab includes information about the document Metadata contained in the file.

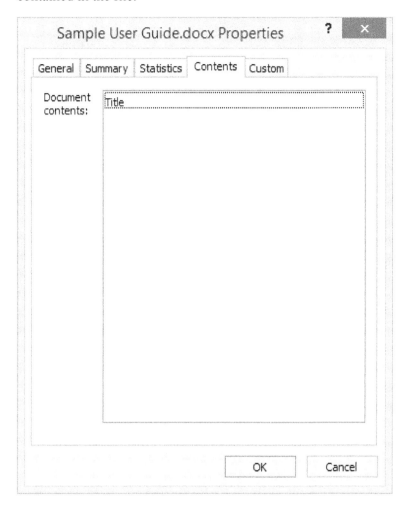

The Custom tab allows you to add custom properties to your document. To add a custom property, complete the following steps.

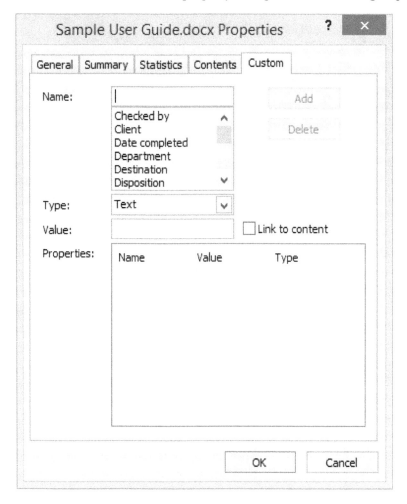

Step 1: Select a **Name** from the list or enter your own name.

Step 2: Select the **Type** of information from the drop down list.

Step 3: Enter the **Value** for the information.

Step 4: Select **Add**.

To review the Document information panel, use the following procedure.

Step 1: Select the arrow next to **Properties**.

Step 2: Select **Show Document Panel** from the drop down list. The Document Information panel opens below the Ribbon, where you can quickly fill in the information.

Chapter 2 – Working with Reusable Content

Microsoft Word has many ways to reuse content, such as small snippets of text or even images and whole pages of formatting. This chapter will start by looking at Autotext, which is a type of Quick Part in Word. Then you'll learn how to insert a Quick Part. This module also explains how to create customized building blocks to really help save you time. Finally, you'll learn how to edit a building block.

Saving Selection as Autotext

To create an Autotext entry, use the following procedure.

Step 1: Select the text you want to store.

Step 2: Select the **Insert** tab from the Ribbon.

Step 3: Select **Quick Parts**.

Step 4: Select **AutoText** from the drop down list.

Step 5: Select **Save Selection to AutoText Gallery**.

3. → Select·a·**Zoom·to**·option.¶

Step 6: In the *Create New Building Block* dialog box, enter a **Name** for the AutoText entry.

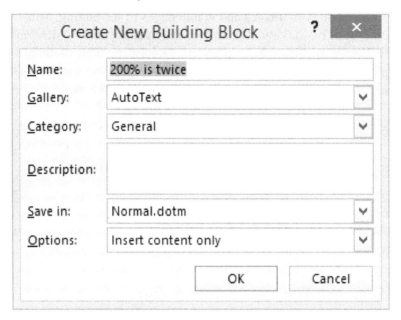

Step 7: Keep the **Gallery** as AutoText.

Step 8: Select a **Category** from the drop down list. You can also create a new category to help organize your AutoText entries.

Step 9: Enter a **Description**, if desired, to explain the purpose of your AutoText entry.

Step 10: Select the template where you would like to save the AutoText entry from the **Save in** drop down list. Remember that Normal is the template used when you create a new blank document.

Step 11: Select an item from the **Options** drop down list. In most cases, you'll use **Insert Content Only**.

Step 12: Select **OK**.

Inserting a Quick Part

To insert a Quick Part, use the following procedure.

Step 1: Place your cursor where you want the reusable content to appear.

Step 2: Select the **Insert** tab from the Ribbon.

Step 3: Select **Quick Parts**.

Step 4: Select the Quick Part that you want to use from the Gallery. Or select **AutoText** and select the AutoText entry that you want to use from the AutoText Gallery.

The selected item is inserted at your cursor position.

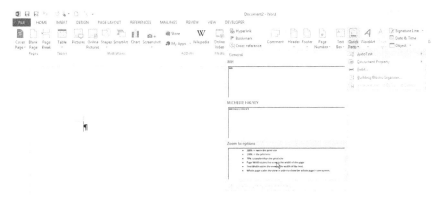

Creating Customized Building Blocks

To create a building block, use the following procedure.

Step 1: Find the item you want to save as a building block and select it.

Step 2: Select the **Insert** tab from the Ribbon.

Step 3: Select **Quick Parts**.

Step 4: Select **Save Selection to Quick Part Gallery** from the drop down list.

- → 200%·is·twice·the·print·size.¶
- → 100%·is·the·print·size.¶
- → 75%·is·smaller·than·the·print·size.¶

Step 5: In the *Create New Building Block* dialog box, enter a **Name** for the Building Block.

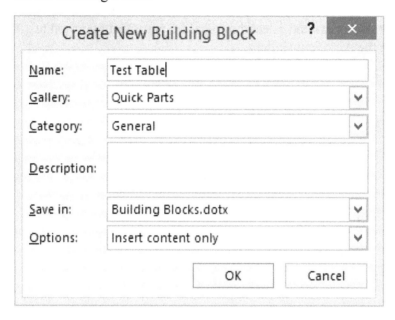

Step 6: Select a **Gallery** from the drop down list. For example, if your building block is a footer, you can place it in the Footers gallery. However, in most cases, the default setting of Quick Parts is fine.

Step 7: Select a **Category** from the drop down list. You can also create a new category to help organize your Building Blocks.

Step 8: Enter a **Description**, if desired, to explain the purpose of your Building Block.

Step 9: Select the template where you would like to save the Building Block from the **Save in** drop down list. Remember that Normal is the template used when you create a new blank document.

Step 10: Select an item from the **Options** drop down list. In most cases, you'll use **Insert Content Only**.

Step 11: Select **OK**.

Editing a Building Block

To review the Building Block Organizer, use the following procedure.

Step 1: Select the **Insert** tab from the Ribbon.

Step 2: Select **Quick Parts**.

Step 3: Select **Building Block Organizer** from the drop down list.

The Building Blocks Organizer lists all of the Building Blocks that are associated with the template you are using for the current document. There are many built-in Building Blocks associated with themes and other items.

You can click on the headers at the top of the list to sort the items by Name, Gallery, Category, or Template. When you select a Building Block the right side of the window displays a preview of the Building Block.

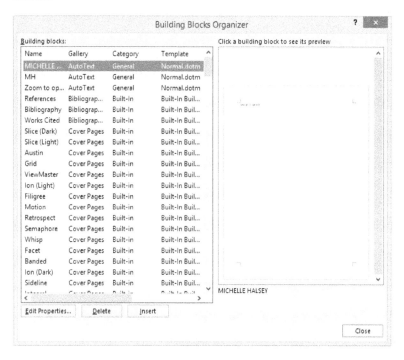

To delete a Building Block, highlight it in the list and select **Delete**.

To insert a Building Block, highlight it in the list and select **Insert**.

To edit the properties of a Building Block, use the following procedure.

Step 1: In the *Building Blocks Organizer* window, highlight the Building Block you want to edit, and select **Edit Properties**.

Step 2: In the Modify Building Blocks dialog box, edit the **Name**, **Gallery**, **Category**, **Description**, **Template** location, or **Options**.

Step 3: To create a new Category, select the **Category** drop down list. Select **Create New Category**.

Step 4: In the *Create New Category* dialog box, enter a new **Name** for the Category. Select **OK**.

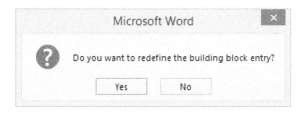

Step 5: In the *Modify Building Block* dialog box, select **OK**.

Step 6: Word displays a warning message to make sure that you want to redefine the Building Block. Select **Yes** to continue.

To correct a Building Block by saving over the original, use the following procedure.

Step 1: Insert the Quick Part you want to change into your document.

Step 2: Make the content and/or formatting changes that you want to make.

Step 3: Select the content to include in the corrected Quick Part.

Step 4: Select the **Insert** tab from the Ribbon.

Step 5: Select **Quick Parts**.

Step 6: Select **Save Selection to Quick Part Gallery** from the drop down list.

Step 7: In the *Create New Building Block* dialog box, enter a **Name** for the Building Block. Make sure that the name is the same as the item you are correcting.

Step 8: Select the **Gallery, Category**, **Description**, **Save in** location, and **Options** as when you created the Building Block originally.

Step 9: Select **OK**.

Step 10: Word displays a warning message to make sure that you want to overwrite the Building Block entry. Select **Yes** to continue.

Chapter 3 – Working with Templates

Templates can be a huge time saver for occasions when you need to make many documents with the same types of formatting. In this module, you'll learn about using templates in Word 2013. Then you'll learn how to modify an existing template. You'll also learn how to create a new template. This module explains how to apply a template to an existing document so that you can quickly reformat a document. Finally, you'll learn how to manage your templates.

About Templates

Templates provide a consistent, familiar look to your documents. It is a convenient, time-saving way to create documents rather than modifying another document or starting from scratch each time. You may already be familiar with using the templates provided by Word.

Did you know that these templates could be modified so that you can create multiple documents from the modified template? You may want to start with a design from an Office.com template, but customize it for your purposes. Then you can create multiple documents from the modified template.

You can also create your own template. This allows you to completely customize the blueprint for the documents that will be based on your template. You can customize everything about the template, creating placeholders for styles, spacing and other design elements instead of adding content to the document.

Finally, you can even reformat a document that has already been created by applying a new template to the document. In this way, you can use different branding for different scenarios for the same document.

Here are some important tips to remember to maximize the benefit of using templates.

- Use Global settings instead of local ones. Global settings are the settings that affect the entire document (or most of it), such as themes and styles. Local settings are those that you have applied to a single object or paragraph. Just remember that you can quickly reformat a document by changing a style if styles were used consistently throughout the document. If the style is in the template from the beginning, it makes the formatting (or reformatting) that much easier.

- Similarly, use alignment and indents for paragraph spacing instead of using tabs or spaces. Tabs and spaces can cause problems when you replace placeholder text in a template with other content.

- Use tables for positioning items like graphics. Again, your spacing can be changed when you replace placeholder content with real content. Use a table with no borders instead and the spacing will stay the same for every document based on that template.

Modifying an Existing Template

To modify an existing template, use the following procedure.

Step 1: Open the file that you want to modify. The templates are stored in the following location:
C:\Users\user name\App Data\Roaming\Microsoft\Templates

Step 2: If there are not any files listed, select the **Files** drop down list and select Document Templates.

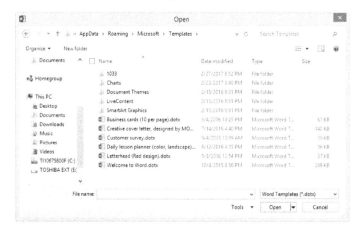

Step 3: Highlight the file you want to modify and select **Open**.

Step 4: Make the changes you want to have applied to future documents based on this template, including styles, page layouts, placeholder content, etc.

Step 5: Save the file.

Creating a New Template

To create a template, use the following procedure.

Step 1: Create a new, blank document.

Step 2: Make the changes you want to have applied to future documents based on this template, including styles, page layouts, placeholder content, etc. You can control any settings for the template to create consistency in future documents based on this template.

Step 3: Select the **File** tab from the Ribbon to open the Backstage View.

Step 4: Select **Save As**.

Step 5: Navigate to the following location in the Save As dialog box: **C:\Users\user name\App Data\Roaming\Microsoft\Templates**

Step 6: Select Word Template or Macro-Enabled Word template (dotx or dotm) from the **Save as Type** drop down list.

Step 7: Select **Save**.

Applying a Template to an Existing Document

To apply a template to an existing document, use the following procedure.

Step 1: Open the document you want to reformat.

Step 2: Open the *Options* dialog box by selecting Options from the Backstage View.

Step 3: Select the **Add Ins** tab.

Step 4: Select the **Manage** drop down list. Select **Templates** from the list of options.

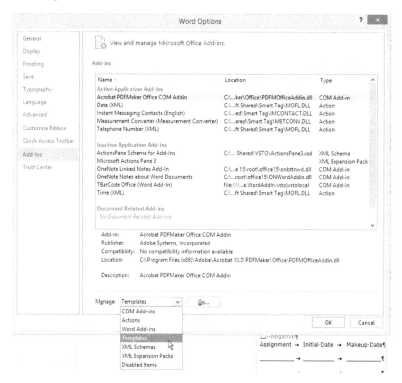

Step 5: Select **Go**.

Step 6: In the *Templates and Add-Ins* Window, select **Attach**.

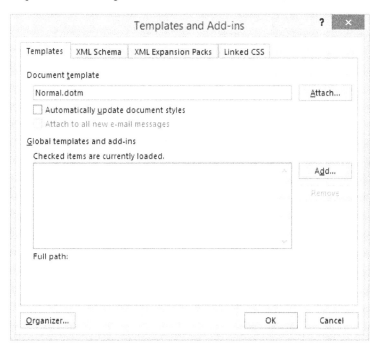

Step 7: In the *Attach Template* dialog box, navigate to the location of the template you want to apply. Highlight it and select **Open**.

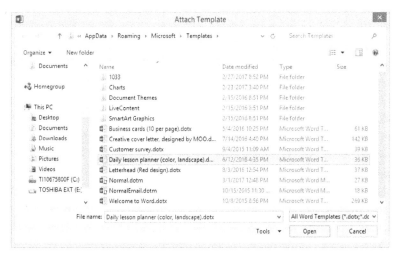

Step 8: In the *Templates and Add-ins* window, check the **Automatically update document styles** box to reformat the document using the templates styles.

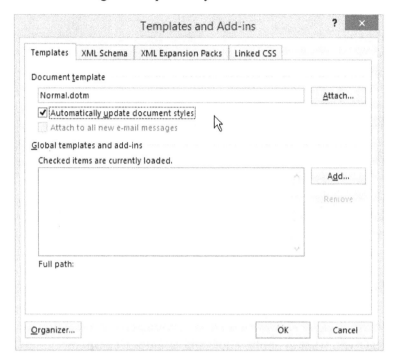

Step 9: Select **OK.**

The document is reformatted according to the themes, styles, and page layouts applied in the document and available in the template.

Managing Templates

To load additional template items to the current document, use the following procedure.

Step 1: Open the document you want to reformat.

Step 2: Open the *Options* dialog box by selecting Options from the Backstage View.

Step 3: Select the **Add Ins** tab.

Step 4: Select the **Manage** drop down list. Select **Templates** from the list of options.

Step 5: Select **Go**.

Step 6: In the *Templates and Add-Ins* Window, select **Add**.

Step 7: In the *Add template* dialog box, select the template that contains the items you want to load to the current document. Select **OK**.

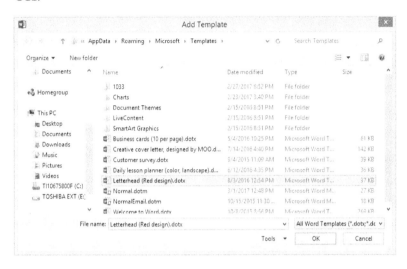

Step 8: The item is listed in the *Templates and Add-ins* window. Select **OK** to continue working in your document using the newly loaded items.

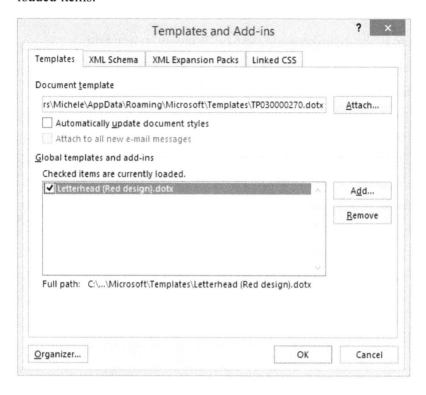

To use the Organizer, use the following procedure.

Step 1: In the *Templates and Add-ins* window, select **Organizer**.

The *Organizer* window includes two files at a time. The left side lists the styles available in the file listed in the **Styles available in** drop down list. The right side lists the styles available in the file listed in the **Styles available** drop down list on the right side. On either side, you can select a new file from the list. You can also close a selected file. When all of the files are closed, you can open a new one.

To copy styles from one file to another, highlight the style on the left side, and select **Copy**. You can also highlight a style and **delete** it or **rename** it. Select **Close** when you have finished working in the *Organizer* window.

Chapter 4 – Working with Sections and Linked Content

In this chapter, you'll learn some powerful uses for sections. First, we'll take a general look at sections and learn how to enter a section break. Next, we'll cover how to customize page numbers in a document using sections. Then we'll look at using multiple page formats in a document. This module also explains how to use different headers and footers in a document. Finally, we'll take a look at how to link and unlink text boxes.

Using Sections

To insert a section into a document, use the following procedure.

Step 1: Place the cursor in the location where you want to split the document. The new section will begin where the cursor is located.

Step 2: Select the **Page Layout** tab from the Ribbon.

Step 3: Select the type of **Section Break** from the drop down list.

Step 3a: **Next Page** – select this option to start the section on the next page. You'll need this one if you want to use the section to create different page layouts within the document.

Step 3b: **Continuous** – select this option to start the section immediately. You might use this one if you want to include different column layouts within the same page.

Step 3c: **Even Page** – select this option if you are using a two-page layout and you want the next section to start on an even page. A blank page will be inserted if necessary.

Step 3d: **Odd Page** – select this option if you are using a two-page layout and you want the next section to start on an add page. A blank page will be inserted if necessary.

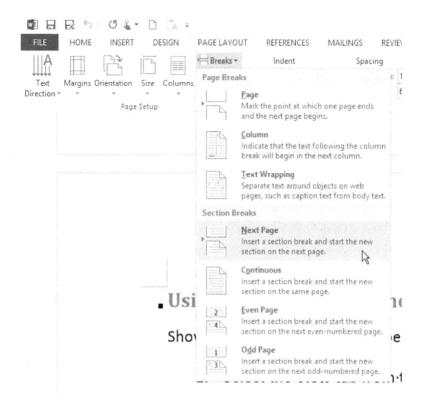

Customizing Page Numbers in Sections

To create custom page numbers, use the following procedure.

Step 1: Double-click in the footer area of the first section to open the **Header & Footer Tools Design** tab on the Ribbon.

Step 2: If the **Link to Previous** option is active (in the Navigation group), select it to turn it off. Customized page numbers do not work if the sections are linked.

Step 3: Enter the page number in the desired location by selecting **Page Number** and select the desired option from the drop down list.

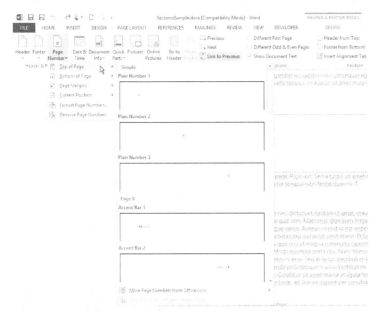

Step 4: Select **Format Page Numbers** from the **Page Number** drop down list to open the *Page Number Format* dialog box.

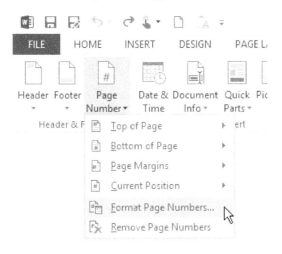

Step 5: Select the **Number Format** from the drop down list.

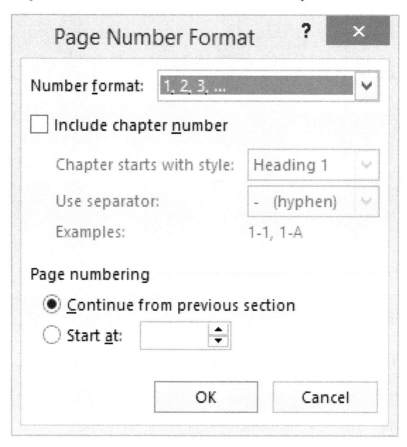

Step 6: Select **Start at** and enter the starting page number for this section.

Page Number Format

Number format: i, ii, iii, ...

☐ Include chapter number

Chapter starts with style: Heading 1

Use separator: - (hyphen)

Examples: 1-1, 1-A

Page numbering

○ Continue from previous section

● Start at: i

OK   Cancel

Step 7: Select **OK**.

Step 8: Make sure there is a section break at the end of the current section. Move to the next section's footer. If the **Link to Previous** option is active (in the Navigation group), select it to turn it off. You may need to unlink each section separately.

Step 9: Select **Format Page Numbers** from the **Page Number** drop down list to open the *Page Number Format* dialog box for this section.

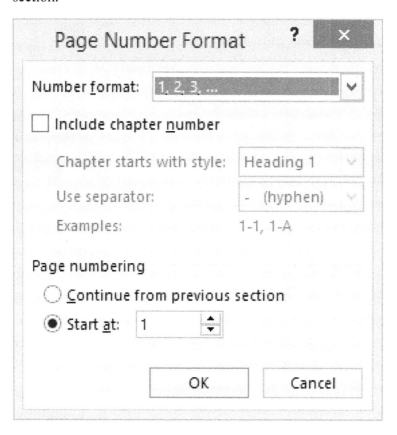

Step 10: Choose the **Number format** and the **Page numbering** start location for this and select **OK** to apply the formatting to this section's page numbering.

Using Multiple Page Formats in a Document

To add a landscape section to a document that is portrait oriented, use the following procedure.

Step 1: Create a section break at the end of the document.

Step 1a: Select the **Page Layout** tab on the Ribbon.

Step 1b: Select **Breaks**.

Step 1c: Select **Next Page**.

Step 2: Making sure that the cursor is located AFTER the section break, open the *Page Layout* dialog box by selecting the small square in the **Page Setup** group of the **Page Layout** tab on the Ribbon.

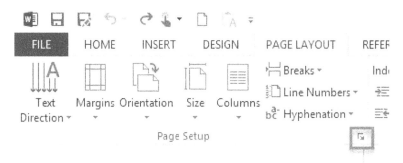

Step 3: On the *Margins* tab, select **Landscape** as the orientation.

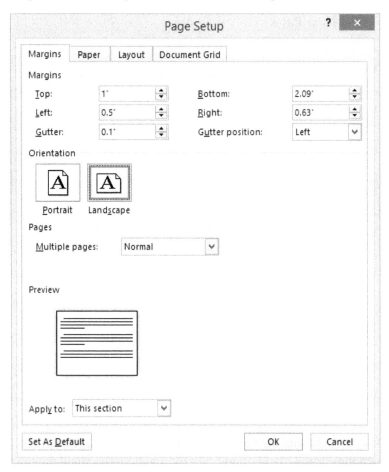

Step 4: In the **Apply To** list at the bottom, make sure that **This Section** is selected from the drop down list.

Step 5: Select **OK**.

Chapter·2:··
Samnla·Tamnlata¶

The new section has a different page orientation.

Using Different Headers and Footers in a Document

To use different headers and footers using sections, use the following procedure.

Step 1: Double-click in the header area of the first section to open the **Header & Footer Tools Design** tab on the Ribbon.

Step 2: In this example, the Title Page should not have headers or footers, so we'll check the **Different First Page** box. Select **Go to Footer** and check the **Different First Page** box for it.

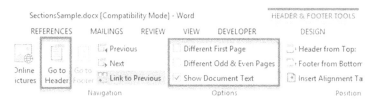

Step 3: If the **Link to Previous** option is active (in the Navigation group), select it to turn it off. It is highlighted if it is active. The Link to Previous option makes the active header or footer the same as the previous section's header or footer. You'll need to unlink headers and footers separately.

Step 4: Make sure there is a section break at the end of the current section. Move to the next section's header or footer. If the **Link to Previous** option is active (in the Navigation group), select it to turn it off. You may need to unlink each section separately.

Step 5: Enter the header and/or footer information that is different from the previous section.

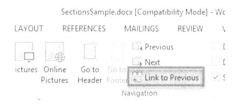

Linking and Breaking Links for Text Boxes

Use the following procedure to link text boxes.

Step 1: In the sample document, scroll to the text box on page two.

Step 2: Select the text box by clicking on it.

Step 3: Select the **Text Box Tools Format** tab on the Ribbon.

Step 4: Select **Create Link**.

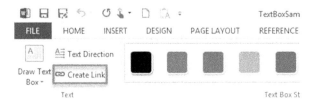

Notice how the cursor changes to a pitcher. This indicates that you are creating a text box link, and there is text to flow to an empty text box.

Step 5: Click on the empty text box where you want the text to flow. Notice how the cursor changes to a pouring pitcher when you mouse over an empty text box.

Step 6: The text boxes are now linked. Extra text from the first text box flows into the second text box.

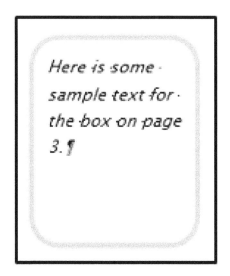

To break a link, return to the first text box. When you select the text box, the Break Link option becomes available.

Chapter 5 – Managing Versions and Tracking Documents

Word 2013 has some great features to help you work with your documents. If you need to go back to an earlier version, you can use the auto save feature to help you restore an earlier version. This module explains how to configure your auto save settings so that previous versions of your documents will be available. It also explains how to review, compare, and restore previous versions. You'll also learn how to work with tracked comments and changes from multiple authors. First, you'll learn how to combine the changes and comments into one document. Then, you can use that compilation to review all of the comments at one time.

Merging Different Versions of a Document

To configure the auto-save settings, use the following procedure.

Step 1: Select the **File** tab from the Ribbon to display the Backstage view.

Step 2: Select **Options**.

Step 3: In the *Word Options* dialog box, select the **Save** tab.

Step 4: Check the **Save AutoRecover information every __ minutes** box to enable the auto save feature.

Step 5: Enter a number of minutes in between auto saves in the box, or you can use the up and down arrows to adjust the number of minutes.

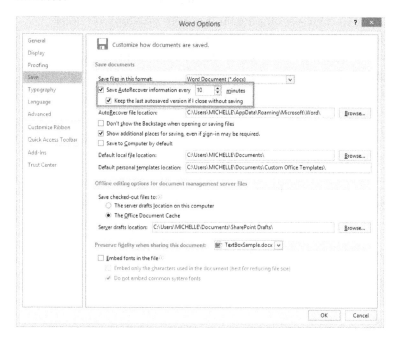

Step 6: Select **OK**.

To view the Versions on the Backstage view, select the **File** tab on the Ribbon. Make sure that the Info tab on the Backstage view is selected.

You can click on a version to open it as a separate file. A message appears at the top of the file that indicates it is an AutoSaved version.

Select **Compare** to open a new file with changes marked between the version you selected and the original file you have open.

Select **Restore** to return the selected version to the original file you have open.

To recover an unsaved document, use the following procedure.

Step 1: Select the **File** tab from the Ribbon to display the Backstage view.

Step 2: On the **Info** tab, select **Manage Versions**. Select **Recover Unsaved Documents**.

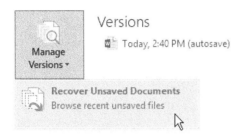

Step 3: In the *Open* dialog box, any auto-saved files that can be recovered are shown in the default location. Select the one you want to recover and select **Open**.

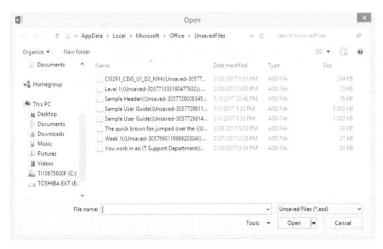

Tracking Comments in a Combined Document

To merge comments and changes from several documents into one document, use the following procedure.

Step 1: The file where you want to combine your changes should be open.

Step 2: Select the **Review** tab from the Ribbon.

Step 3: Select **Compare**. Select **Combine** from the drop down list.

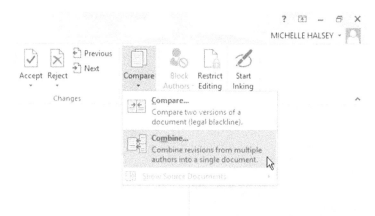

Step 4: In the **Original document** area, select the name of the document where you want to combine the changes from multiple sources. If it isn't open, select the folder to open the file.

Step 5: Make sure that any changes in this document are marked with a name or initials by entering the desired **Label**.

Step 6: Under **Revised document**, select the name of the document where the changes are from the drop down list (if the file is open). Otherwise, select the folder to open the file.

Step 7: Make sure that any changes in this document are marked with a name or initials by entering the desired **Label**.

Step 8: If you need to switch the documents (you have the document with revisions as the original), select the double arrow icon.

Step 9: Select **More** to see all of the **Comparison Settings**.

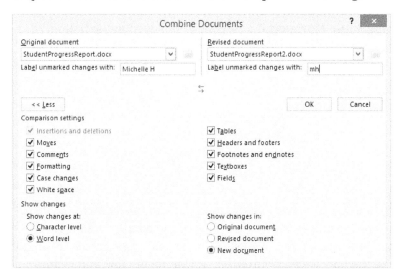

Step 10: Check the box(es) to indicate which items to include in the comparison.

Step 11: Indicate whether you want to show changes at the Character or Word level. For example, if the word cat is changes to cats, Word shows the entire word changed instead of just the letter s by default.

Step 12: Indicate whether to show the changes in the original document, the revised document, or a new document.

Step 13: Select **OK**.

Step 14: For multiple authors, repeat steps 1-13 until you have merged all of the changes into a single document.

Reviewing Comments in a Combined Document

To review the comments in the combined documents, use the following procedure.

Step 1: In the document where the comments have been combined, select the **Review** tab from the Ribbon.

Step 2: Select **Reviewing Pane**. Select **Reviewing Pane Vertical** to see the comments on the left side of the Word window. Select **Reviewing Pane Horizontal** to see the comments on the bottom of the Word window.

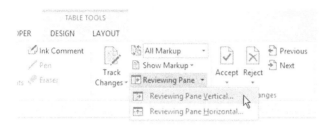

Step 3: The Revisions pane color codes the comments, with the name or initials of the author on the right side of the comment/change heading. Each change or comment is marked with the type of change requested, such as Deleted, Inserted, or Comment. You can make edits right in the Revisions pane.

Step 4: You can also see the comments in bubbles on the right side of the Word window. Remember that you can respond to comments right in the Comments window.

Chapter 6 – Using Cross References

In this chapter, you'll learn how to use cross references to guide your reader to other information in your document. First, we'll learn about the different types of cross references. Then, you'll learn how to insert a bookmark to use as a cross reference. This module explains how to insert a cross reference to a bookmark or to heading text. You'll also learn how to update a cross reference. Finally, we'll take a look at some advanced tools to use in formatting your cross references.

Types of Cross References

Discuss the different types of cross references.

- **Numbered items** – references a selected paragraph number.

- **Headings** – references a selected paragraph formatted with a heading style.

- **Bookmarks** – references a bookmark location you have inserted into the document.

- **Footnotes** – references a selected footnote.

- **Endnotes** – references a selected endnote.

- **Equations** – references a selected equation.

- **Figures** – references a selected figure.

- **Tables** – references a selected table.

Inserting a Bookmark

To insert a bookmark, use the following procedure.

Step 1: Place your cursor in the location where you want to insert the bookmark.

Step 2: Select the **Insert** tab from the Ribbon.

Step 3: Select **Bookmark**.

Step 4: In the *Bookmark* dialog box, enter a **Bookmark Name** for your location. This name will help you find this location later.

Step 5: Select **Add**.

Inserting a Cross Reference

To insert a cross reference, use the following procedure.

Step 1: Place your cursor in the location where you want to insert the cross reference.

Step 2: Select the **Insert** tab from the Ribbon.

Step 3: Select **Cross-reference**.

Step 4: In the *Cross-reference* dialog box, select the **Reference type** from the drop down list. In this example, we'll choose the Bookmark we created in the previous lesson.

Step 5: Select the bookmark you want to use from the **For which bookmark** list.

Step 6: Select the type of information you want to reference from the **Insert reference to** drop down list. In this case, we want to use the page number.

65

Step 7: Select **Insert**.

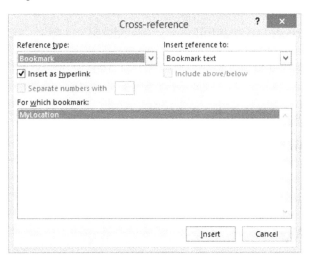

To insert a cross reference that includes heading text, use the following procedure.

Step 1: Place your cursor in the location where you want to insert the cross reference.

Step 2: Select the **Insert** tab from the Ribbon.

Step 3: Select **Cross-reference**.

Step 4: In the *Cross-reference* dialog box, select the **Reference type** from the drop down list. In this example, we'll choose a heading.

Step 5: Select the heading you want to use from the **For which Heading** list.

Step 6: Select the type of information you want to reference from the **Insert reference to** drop down list. In this case, we want to use the heading text.

Step 7: Select **Insert**.

Cross-reference

Reference type:

Heading

☑ Insert as hyperlink

☐ Separate numbers with

For which heading:

CONTENTS
OUR UPCOMING PLANS TO TRAVEL TO EUROPE FOR THE SUMMER

Insert reference to:

Heading text

☐ Include above/below

Insert   Cancel

Updating a Cross Reference

To update a single cross reference, use the following procedure.

Step 1: Right-click the cross reference text. The cross reference text will be highlighted in gray when you select it or right-click on it.

Step 2: Select **Update Field** from the context menu.

To update all fields in a document at once, use the following procedure.

Step 1: Press Ctrl + A to select all text in the document.

Step 2: Press F9.

Step 3: If the document has a Table of Contents or other special types of fields, you may get a confirmation message to clarify how you want to update the fields.

Note that using this method does not update fields in the header or footer. You will need to select cross references placed there separately.

Formatting Cross References Using Fields

Review the *Field* dialog box. To open it, right-click on a field and select **Edit Field** from the context menu.

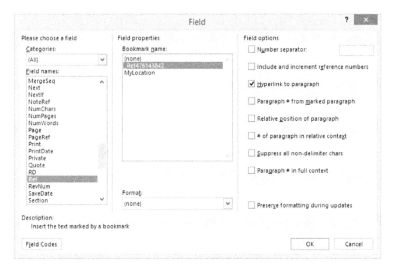

The current Field Name is selected with the Field properties, such as the location it references. The Field options include additional ways you can control the field, including:

- Number separator

- Include and increment reference numbers

- Hyperlink to paragraph

- Paragraph # from marked paragraph

- Relative position of paragraph

- # of paragraph in relative context

- Suppress all non-delimiter chars

- Paragraph # in full context

- Preserve formatting during updates

The Format drop down list allows you to control the case of the reference.

The Field Options are different, depending on what type of field you are editing.

Select **Field Codes** to open the **Advanced field properties** area where you can edit the actual coding.

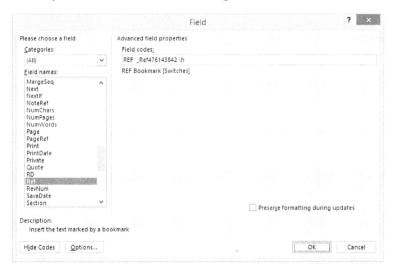

Select **Options** to see the switches.

The *General Switches* tab includes the same case formatting options you've seen previously. When you select an option, you can see the description at the bottom. Select **Add to Field** to include the switch with the field code.

The *Field Specific Switches* tab includes additional options, based on what type of field you have selected. When you select an option, you can see the description at the bottom. Select **Add to Field** to include the switch with the field code.

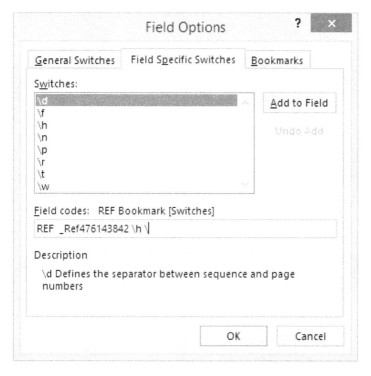

Select **OK** to close the *Field Options* dialog box.

Chapter 7 – Creating Mail Merges and Labels

This chapter explains how to use mail merges to create customized letters, emails and labels. You'll learn how to create a mail merge with an external data source. Then you'll learn how to create a custom merge by entering a new list of data for barcodes. This module also explains how to create return address labels using the Labels option. Finally, you'll learn about using Avery Label Templates.

Creating a Mail Merge

To create a mail merge, use the following procedure.

Step 1: Open the document that contains the letter you want to personalize in a mail merge.

Step 2: Select the **Mailings** tab from the Ribbon.

Step 3: Select Start **Mail Merge**. Select **Step by Step Mail Merge Wizard** from the drop down list.

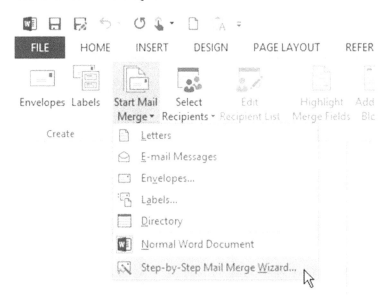

Step 4: The *Mail Merge* pane opens on the right side of the screen.

Step 5: Indicate the **Document Type** you want to use. In this example, we'll keep Letter selected. Note that you can create emails, envelopes, letters, or a directory.

Step 6: Select **Next** at the bottom of the Mail Merge pane.

Step 7: Indicate which **Starting Document** you want to use. In this example, we'll use the Current Document.

Step 8: Select **Next**.

Step 9: Select the **Recipients**. In this example, we'll use an existing Excel file.

Step 10: Select **Browse** to open the file.

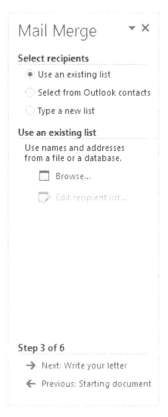

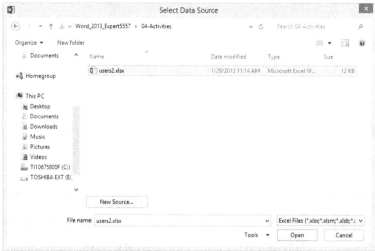

Step 11: Select the location of the file and select **Open**.

Step 12: Select Table and then select Ok.

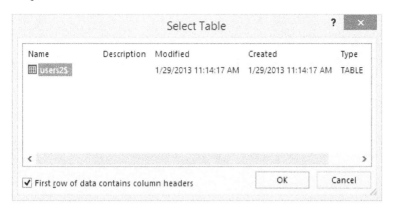

Step 13: The *Mail Merge Recipients* window opens, so that you can see how Word imported the columns. You can select or unselect items. You can also sort, filter, find and validate information. Select **OK**.

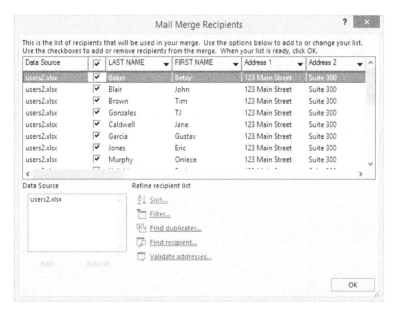

Step 14: Select **Next**.

Step 15: The Write Your Letter step on the wizard allows you to add the personalized details to your letter. Place your cursor in the location on the letter where you want the address to appear. Select **Address Block** to add the contact's address block to the letter.

Step 16: The *Insert Address Block* dialog box appears. You can specify address elements and preview what those details will look like. Select **OK** when you have finished.

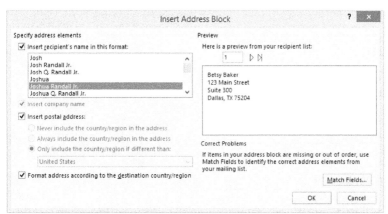

Step 17: Word enters a placeholder for the Address Block.

Step 18: Now let's add a personalized greeting. Move your cursor to the location where you want the greeting. Select **Greeting Line** from the Mail Merge pane.

Step 19: The *Insert Greeting Line* dialog box appears. You can specify the formats and preview what those details will look like. Select **OK** when you have finished.

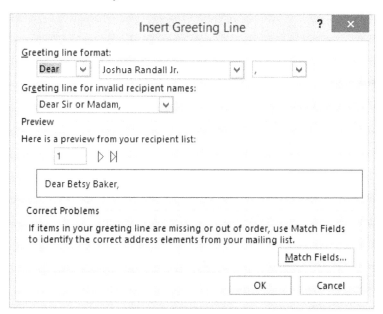

Step 20: Now select **Next** to preview the results. Notice the Tools in the Mailings ribbon to help you navigate through the list. You also can navigate using the Mail Merge pane.

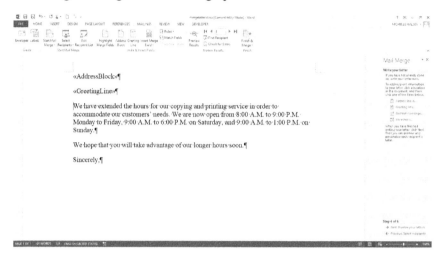

Step 21: Select **Next**.

Step 22: Select **Print** to print your letters.

Step 23: The *Merge to Printer* dialog box allows you to select All, the Current record, or a page range. Select **OK**.

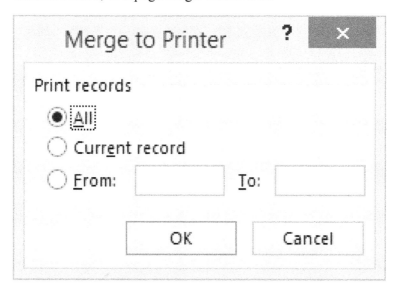

Step 24: The *Print* dialog allows you to control the printing options. Select **OK** when you are ready to print.

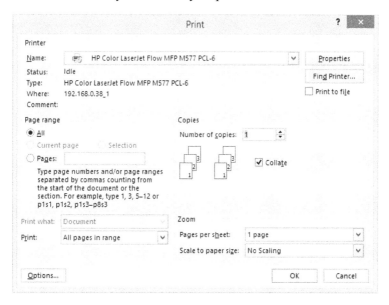

Creating Barcodes

To create a custom mail merge, use the following procedure.

Step 1: Start with a blank document for this example. You can also use an existing document.

Step 2: Select the **Mailings** tab from the Ribbon.

Step 3: Choose **Select Recipients**. Select **Type a New List** from the drop down list.

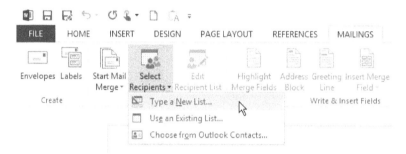

Word displays the *New Address List* dialog box.

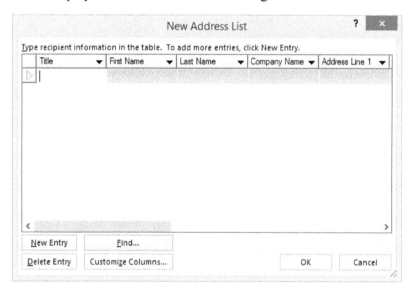

Step 4: You can simply begin typing in your information if you want to use the default columns.

Step 5: To include different information in your list to merge, select Customize Columns.

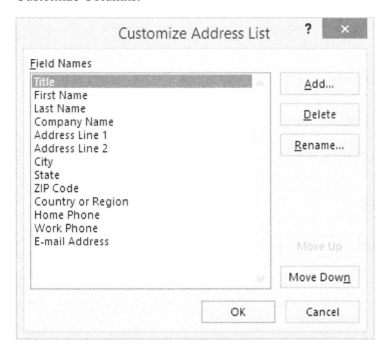

Step 6: The *Customize Address List* dialog box includes the list of default information to include for a merge. You can select any item and select Delete to remove that column from the list. You can also select an item and select Rename to change the name for that item. You can reorganize the list by selecting Move Up or Move Down.

Step 7: To create a new type of information (such as a barcode number), select Add.

Step 8: Enter the name of the column in the *Add Field* dialog box and select OK.

Step 9: When you have finished customizing your columns, select OK in the *Customize Address List* dialog box.

Step 10: Enter the data for each record in the *New Address List* dialog box.

Step 11: In the *Save Address List* dialog box, enter a File name for the list. The default location to save the list is in My Data Sources. However, you can also select a new location, if desired. Select Save.

Note that at any time, you can choose Use Existing List from the Select Recipients command on the Mailings tab of the Ribbon to open that file.

Once you have selected your recipients, you are ready to write and insert your merge fields.

The Write & Insert Fields group in the Mailings tab includes the most commonly used merge fields: Address Block and Greeting Line. You've seen these in the previous lesson. The Insert Merge Field list includes the items you customized in the *Customize Address List* dialog box. It allows you to insert an individual field separately. Practice inserting these fields, if desired.

Step 12: Select the Insert Barcode Field option to generate barcodes from the information in the selected field.

Step 13: In the *Select a Field and Barcode Type* dialog box, first select that Field in your data source contains the barcode information. This should be the field that you created in Step 7 and the records that you entered in Step 10.

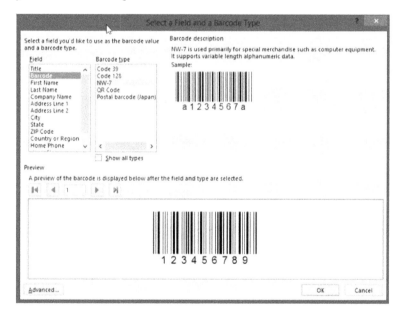

Step 14: Select the Barcode type from the next list. When you select each option, you can view a description on the right and a preview at the bottom. For the preview, you can navigate using the buttons to go to the first record, the previous record, a specific record number, the next record, or the last record.

Step 15: To format the barcode, select Advanced.

Step 16: Each type of barcode has a different *Advanced option* dialog box. However, they all allow some formatting. Select OK when you have finished formatting the barcodes.

When you have finished inserting your fields, you can use the Preview Results option to see your finished document, ready for merging.

Step 17: Select Finish & Merge to finalize your mail merge. Select Print Documents. You'll use the same Merge to Printer dialog and Print dialog as in the previous lesson.

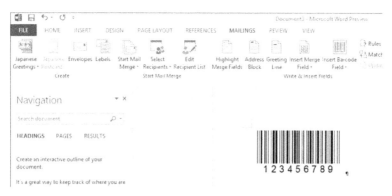

Creating Return Address Labels

To store their return addresses and introduce the Envelopes option, use the following procedure.

Step 1: Select the Mailings tab from the Ribbon.

Step 2: Select Envelopes.

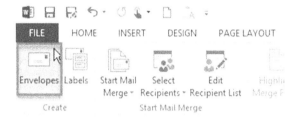

Step 3: In the Return Address area, enter your return address.

Step 4: Select Add to Document.

When Word prompts you to save the default return address, select Yes.

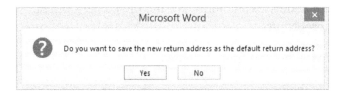

To create a sheet of return address labels, use the following procedure.

Step 1: Select the Mailings tab from the Ribbon.

Step 2: Select Labels.

Step 3: Check the Use Return Address box to display the return address you have previously saved (or if you want to enter a new address and save it as the default return address). You can also just enter the address you want to use in the Address box. You can also choose the Address Book icon to select an address from Outlook.

Step 4: To create a sheet of return address labels, make sure that Full page of the same label is selected.

Step 5: Select Options to choose the type of label you are using. In the *Label Options* dialog box, select the Printer Information, the Label Vendor, and the Product Number.

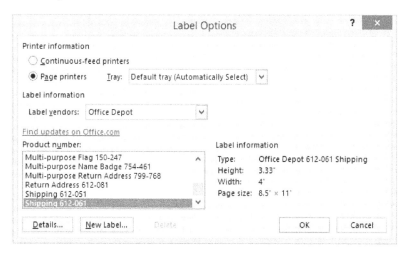

Step 6: You can also customize label dimensions or create your own by selecting Details or New Label. You can enter new measurements in any of the margin or dimension fields. Select OK when you have finished.

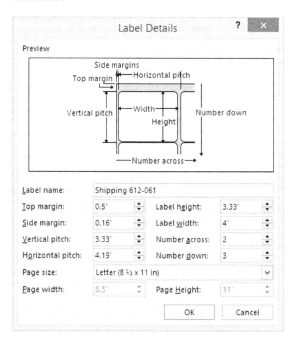

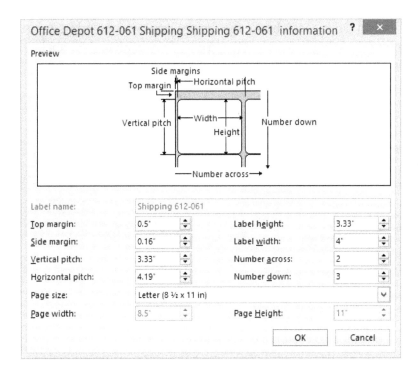

Step 7: Select OK to close the *Label Options* dialog box.

Step 8: In the *Envelopes and Labels* dialog box, you can select either Print to send the plain labels directly to the printer, or you can select New Document to create a document with the appropriate dimensions and information.

If you select a New Document, you can format the labels as desired with font changes or even add small images or other embellishments.

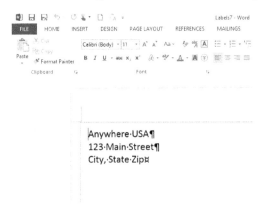

Using Avery Label Templates

To use Avery labels in Word, use the following procedure.

Step 1: Select the File tab to open the Backstage View.

Step 2: Select New.

Step 3: In the Search Online Templates box, enter Avery and press Enter.

Step 4: Select the desired template.

Step 5: Select Create.

Step 6: The document displays with the Avery Template tab displayed. This tab has some additional tools to help you work with the template.

To use the Avery Label template for a sheet of labels that all use the Same Address, use the following procedure.

Step 1: Select Same Address from the Avery ® Template tab.

Step 2: In the *Same Address* dialog box, enter the Name you want to use on the labels.

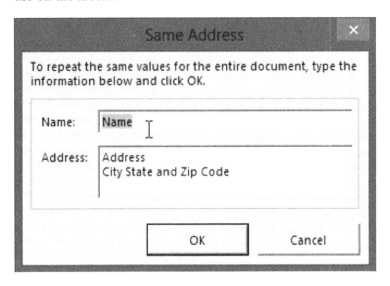

Step 3: Enter the Street address and City, State, and Zip code you want to use on the labels.

Step 4: Select OK.

The labels are updated with the information you added. You can change the alignment (Left, Center, or Right). You can even change, resize, or remove all pictures. If you select a picture, you can choose Change Selected Picture and make one picture different at a time. To print more than one sheet at a time, you can select Add Sheet.

To use the Avery label template for a sheet of labels that use different addresses, use the following procedure.

Step 1: Select Different Addresses.

Step 2: The labels are updated with placeholder text.

Step 3: Replace the text with your addresses.

Chapter 8 – Working with Master Documents

Master documents allow you to keep track of a number of related documents and combine them in a single place to control page numbering, printing, and other activities. In this module, you'll learn how to create a master document and create subdocuments. You'll also learn how to insert a subdocument. Then we'll cover how to work with subdocuments, including expanding and collapsing the subdocuments in the master document, unlinking a subdocument, and merging and splitting subdocuments. Finally, we'll look at how to lock a master document so that changes are not saved in the subdocuments accidentally.

Creating a Master Document

To create a master document, use the following procedure.

Step 1: Start with a blank document.

Step 2: Select the **View** tab from the Ribbon.

Step 3: Select **Outline**.

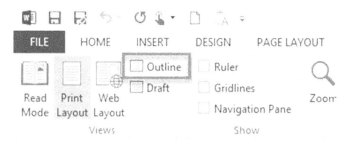

Now you are ready to work with your master document.

Creating Subdocuments

To create subdocuments in a master document, use the following procedure.

Step 1: On the **Outlining** tab of the Ribbon, select **Show Document** to show the tools for working with subdocuments.

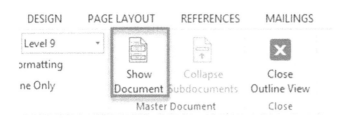

Step 2: Enter some simple headings in your outline view of the sample document, such as:

- Chapter 1

    o Heading 1

    o Heading 2

- Chapter 2

    o Heading 1

    o Heading 2

- Chapter 3

    o Heading 1

    o Heading 2

Step 3: Highlight all of the text.

Step 4: Select **Create** from the **Outlining** tab on the Ribbon.

Step 5: Each "Chapter" becomes its own subdocument. Each subdocument is surrounded by a box and separated by a section break in the master document.

When you save the master document, each subdocument is saved as its own file. The files are named with the text of the heading used at level one for each subdocument.

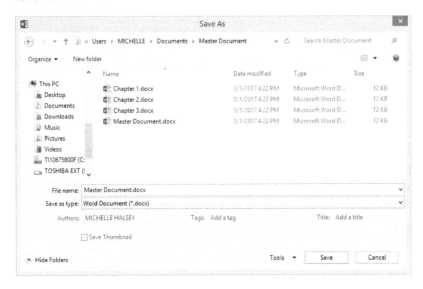

Note that when you make changes to the text from the master document, those changes are also saved in the affected subdocument file.

Inserting a Subdocument

To insert a subdocument, use the following procedure.

Step 1: On the **Outlining** tab of the Ribbon, select **Show Document** to show the tools for working with subdocuments.

Step 2: Select **Insert**.

Step 3: In the *Insert Subdocument* dialog box, navigate to the location of the file you want to use as a subdocument. Highlight it and select **Open**.

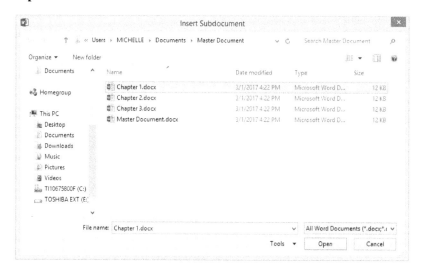

Step 4: If the master document and the subdocument use different templates, you will get a warning message. Select **OK**. Or if they should use the same template, then you will need to go back and use the appropriate template when creating your master document.

Step 5: If the master document and the subdocument use different templates, and they include styles with the same name, but different formatting, you will get an additional warning message. Select Yes to All to rename the styles, or No to All to keep the same names, which will help with reformatting if you are applying a new template.

The subdocument is inserted. Notice that there is a section break automatically inserted at the end of the subdocument.

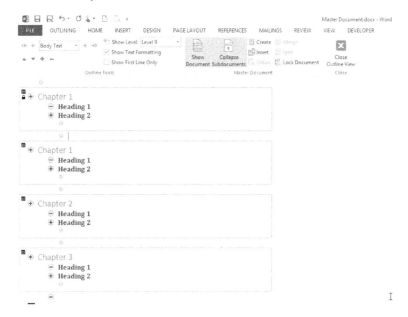

Expanding and Collapsing Subdocuments

To collapse or expand the subdocuments in the master document, use the following procedure.

Step 1: With the text of the subdocuments showing, select **Collapse Subdocuments** from the **Outlining** tab on the Ribbon.

The collapsed view shows the document reference instead of the contents.

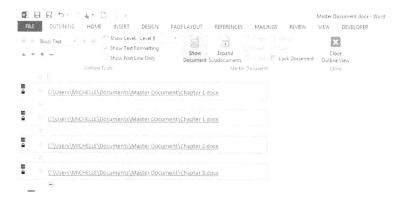

Step 2: With the text of the subdocuments collapsed, select **Expand Subdocuments** from the **Outlining** tab on the Ribbon to see the text again.

Merging and Splitting Subdocuments

To merge subdocuments, use the following procedure.

Step 1: Select the subdocuments in your master document that you want to merge. Notice the small square in the top of each subdocument box. If you click there, it will select the entire subdocument. Hold down the SHIFT or CTRL key to select multiple subdocuments.

Step 2: Select **Merge** from the **Outlining** tab on the Ribbon.

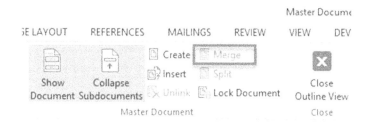

Step 3: Notice that the subdocument icon has been removed from the second subdocument. When you save the master document, the affected subdocuments are also saved.

To split subdocuments, use the following procedure.

Step 1: Select the text in your master document that you want to split from its subdocument into a different subdocument.

Step 2: Select **Split** from the **Outlining** tab on the Ribbon.

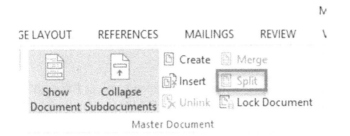

Step 3: Word creates a new subdocument based on the highest level heading of the text you selected.

Unlinking a Subdocument

To unlink a subdocument from a master document, use the following procedure.

Step 1: Select the subdocument that you want to unlink from the master document. Use the little icon at the top left of the subdocument to easily select the whole subdocument.

Step 2: Select **Unlink** from the **Outlining** tab on the Ribbon.

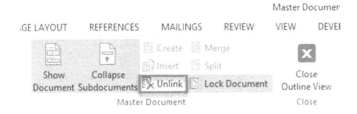

Locking a Master Document

To lock a master document, use the following procedure.

Step 1: Select **Lock Document** from the **Outlining** tab on the Ribbon.

Step 2: Notice the lock icon shown with each subdocument icon.

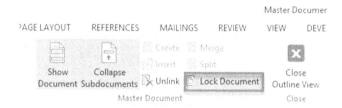

Step 3: To unlock the subdocuments, select **Lock Document** again.

Chapter 9 – Working with Macros

Macros allow you to automate frequently used tasks. You can use macros to speed up routine editing and formatting or combine multiple commands. You can even use a macro to make an option in a dialog box more accessible. This module focuses on learning how to record a macro and how to run a macro. We'll also cover how to apply macro security. Finally, we'll learn how to assign a macro you have recorded to a command button so that it is available from the Ribbon.

Recording a Macro

To record a macro, use the following procedure.

Step 1: Select the **View** tab from the Ribbon.

Step 2: Select **Macros**.

Step 3: Select **Record Macro**.

'ord

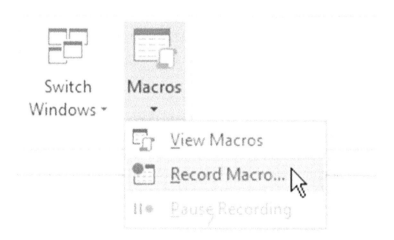

The *Record Macro* dialog box is displayed.

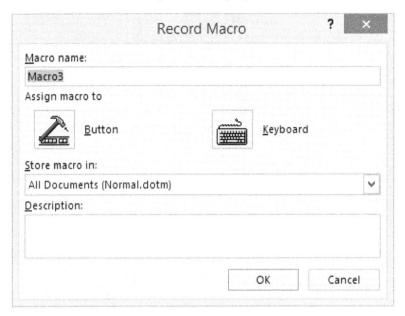

Step 4: Enter a **Name** for your macro. The name cannot contain spaces.

Step 5: Select the location where you would like to **Store** you macro from the drop down list.

Step 6: If desired, enter a **Description** of what your macro accomplishes.

Step 7: Select **OK**.

From this point, every keystroke or command that you perform is recorded. Keep that in mind, so you don't accidentally record things that you don't want performed repetitively. You can type text, perform formatting or insert things like pictures or tables. Just about anything you can do in Word can be recorded in a macro.

Your cursor changes to an icon that looks like a cassette tape...a relic from the first days of macros in previous versions of Word.

Step 8: For this example, insert a table and apply formatting.

Step 9: When you have finished recording your actions, select the **View** tab from the Ribbon again. Select **Macros**. Select **Stop Recording**.

Note that you can also **Pause Recording** to correct something that you don't want as part of your macro, then **Resume Recording** when you are ready.

Running a Macro

To run a macro, use the following procedure.

Step 1: Select the **View** tab from the Ribbon.

Step 2: Select **Macros**.

Step 3: Select View **Macros**.

Vord

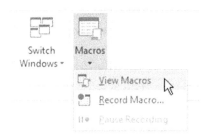

Step 4: In the *Macros* dialog box, select the Macro that you want to run. You can see the **Description** at the bottom to make sure it's the right one.

Step 5: Select **Run**.

Remember that a macro is a series of commands performed separately in the recording, though you get the result almost instantaneously. That means that when you select Undo, it only applies to the last command the macro performed.

Applying Macro Security

To change the macro security, use the following procedure.

Step 1: Select the **File** tab to open the Backstage view.

Step 2: Select **Options**.

Step 3: In the *Word Options* dialog box, select **Trust Center**.

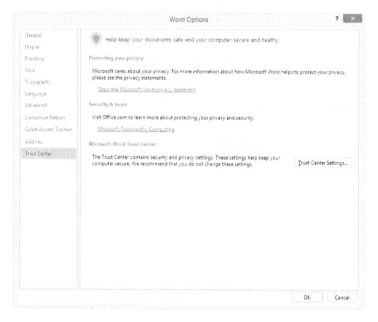

Step 4: Select **Trust Center Settings**.

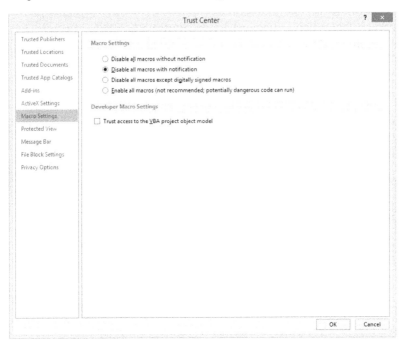

Step 5: In the *Macro settings* area, select the setting you want to use.

Step 6: Select **OK**.

Assigning a Macro to a Command Button or Shortcut Key

To assign a new macro to a command key, use the following procedure.

Step 1: Select the **View** tab from the Ribbon.

Step 2: Select **Macros**.

Step 3: Select **Record Macro**.

The *Record Macro* dialog box is displayed.

Step 1: Enter a **Name** for your macro. The name cannot contain spaces.

Step 2: Enter a **Description** for your macro, if desired.

Step 3: Select **Button**.

Word opens the *Word Options* dialog box, open to the **Quick Access Toolbar** tab.

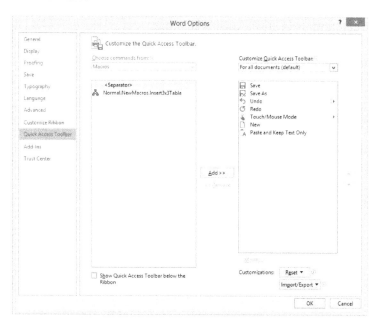

Your Macro is shown in the left list, you can add it to the Quick Access Toolbar by highlighting the macro and selecting **Add**. To change the icon or name, select **Modify**.

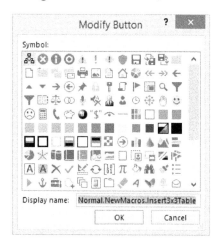

Step 1: Select an icon from the list of **Symbols**.

Step 2: Enter a new **Display name** if desired.

Step 3: Select **OK**.

Now you are recording your macro, as previously learned. Notice the icon you selected in the Quick Access Toolbar.

You can also add the macro to a button on the Ribbon.

Step 1: With the *Word Options* dialog box open (as in the procedure above), select **Customize Ribbon**.

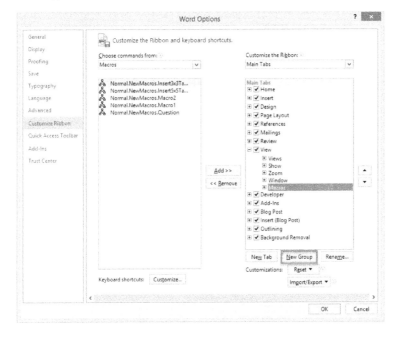

Step 2: Select Macros from the Choose Commands from drop down list.

Your Macros are shown in the left list. You must add a custom group where you will place the button for your macro.

Step 1: Select **New Group**.

Step 2: Select **Rename**.

Step 3: Enter a new **Display name**.

Step 4: Select **OK**.

Now add the macro to the group. Select it in the list on the left and make sure you have your custom group selected on the right.

Step 1: Select **Add**.

Step 2: Select **Rename**.

Step 3: Select an icon for the macro from the list of **Symbols**.

Step 4: Select **OK**.

To assign a new macro to a keyboard shortcut, use the following procedure.

Step 1: Select the **View** tab from the Ribbon.

Step 2: Select **Macros**.

Step 3: Select **Record Macro**.

The *Record Macro* dialog box is displayed.

Step 4: Enter a **Name** for your macro. The name cannot contain spaces.

Step 5: Enter a **Description** for your macro, if desired.

Step 6: Select **Keyboard**.

The *Customize Keyboard* dialog box is displayed.

Step 7: In the **Press new shortcut key** field, press the keys you would like to use for running your macro. If that key is already assigned, it will show the command that key combination is currently used for. You can overwrite a previous association or choose a different key combination. Keys that are pressed at the same time will show a plus sign between them. Keys that are pressed in sequence will show a comma between them.

Step 8: Select **Close**.

Continue recording your macro.

To run the macro, you'll only need to press the shortcut key combination you selected.

Chapter 10 – Working with Forms

In this chapter, you'll learn about forms, where you can make it easy for users to enter specific data without changing the look or spacing of your document. In the first lesson, you'll learn about the Developer tab and creating a form from a template. Then, you'll learn about the form controls, which allow you to add different types of controlled content. This module also explains how to lock a form and add or remove fields. Finally, you'll learn how to insert data from a database onto a form.

Displaying the Developer Tab

The sample form has some areas where the user is asked to change or add information. In the next lesson, we'll learn how to change these to content controls.

To open the Developer tab, use the following procedure.

Step 1: Open the *Options* dialog box by selecting **Options** from the Backstage View.

Step 2: Select the **Customize Ribbon** tab.

Step 3: Check the box next to **Developer**.

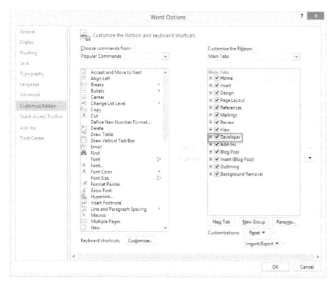

To review the Developer tab hover the mouse over the commands to see the screen tips.

Using Form Controls

To add a text control to a template, use the following procedure.

Step 1: On the **Developer** tab of the Ribbon, select **Design Mode**.

Step 2: Place your cursor in the document template where you want to text control to appear.

Step 3: Select Rich Text Content Control (to allow users to format their text) or the Plain Text Content Control. Word inserts the content control on the document template.

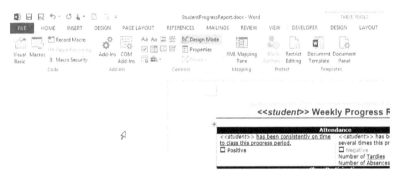

You can format the content control as needed.

Step 4: Make sure to turn off Design Mode when you have finished. Save your changes to the template.

Have the students practice changing items in the sample form to content controls, such as text boxes and check boxes. Turn off Design Mode and practice filling out the form.

Locking and Unlocking a Form

To group the contents of the form, use the following procedure.

Step 1: Select all of the text on the form by pressing Ctrl + A.

Step 2: Select **Group** from the **Developer** tab on the Ribbon.

Step 3: Select **Group**.

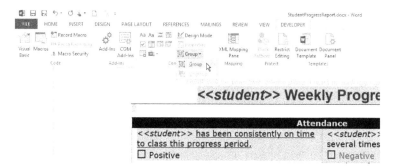

Only the Content Control areas can be changed now.

Step 4: Select **Group** again to remove the grouping.

Use the following procedure to review the Content Control properties.

Step 1: Select the text in a Content Control

Step 2: Select Properties.

Investigate the difference between checking each of the Locking option boxes.

Adding and Removing Fields

To add a field, use the following procedure.

Step 1: Select the **Insert** tab from the Ribbon.

Step 2: Select **Quick Parts**.

Step 3: Select **Form**.

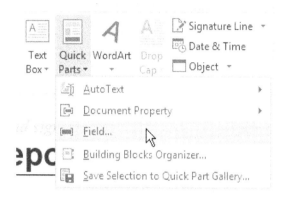

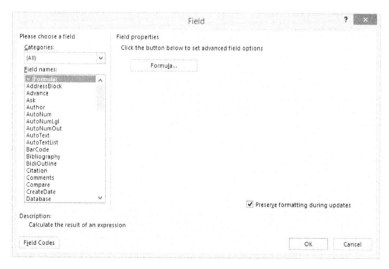

Step 4: In the *Field* dialog box, select the field you want to enter. You can select an option from the **Categories** drop down list to narrow down the options.

Step 5: Adjust the **Field Properties** and **Field Options**, depending on the field that you selected.

Step 6: Select **OK**.

To remove the field, just select it and delete the text.

Linking a Form to a Database

To insert data from a database into a form, use the following procedure.

Step 1: Open the *Options* dialog box by selecting **Options** from the Backstage View.

Step 2: Select the **Customize Ribbon** tab.

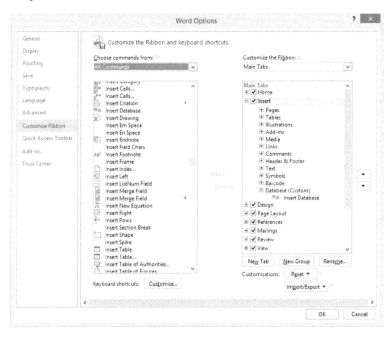

Step 3: In the **Choose Commands From** list, select **Command Not in the Ribbon** from the drop down list.

Step 4: Highlight **Insert Database** from the list.

Step 5: On the **Customize the Ribbon** list, select the **Custom Group** where you want to include the command. See the previous module for information on creating a custom group.

Step 6: Select OK.

Now, with the **Insert Database** command available, select it in the location of your form where you want to include the database records.

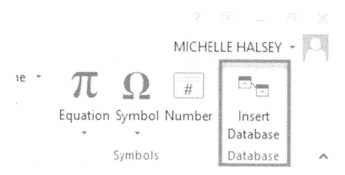

Word displays the *Database* dialog box.

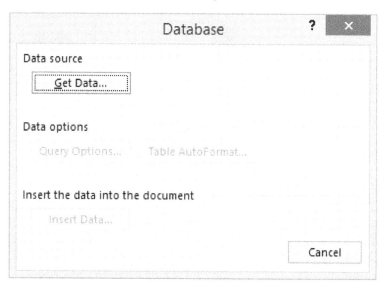

Step 1: Select **Get Data**.

Step 2: In the *Select Data Source* dialog box, navigate to the location of the database you want to use. Highlight it and select **Open**.

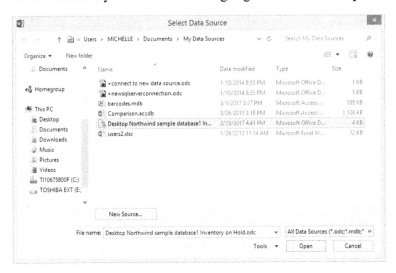

Step 3: If your database contains more than one table, the *Select Table* dialog box appears. Highlight the table you want to use and select **OK**.

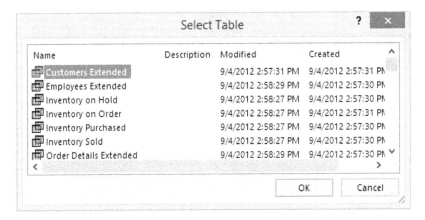

Step 4: Select Insert Data in the *Database* dialog box to choose records to include if you do not want to include all of the records.

Step 5: The *Insert Data* dialog box appears. Select All or indicate the records that you want to include. You can check the **Insert Data as Field checkbox** if desired.

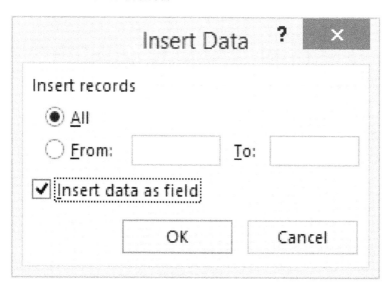

Additional Titles

The Technical Skill Builder series of books covers a variety of technical application skills. For the availability of titles please see https://www.silvercitypublications.com/shop/. Note the Master Class volume contains the Essentials, Advanced, and Expert (when available) editions.

Current Titles

Microsoft Excel 2013 Essentials

Microsoft Excel 2013 Advanced

Microsoft Excel 2013 Expert

Microsoft Excel 2013 Master Class

Microsoft Word 2013 Essentials

Microsoft Word 2013 Advanced

Microsoft Word 2013 Expert

Microsoft Word 2013 Master Class

Microsoft Project 2010 Essentials

Microsoft Project 2010 Advanced

Microsoft Project 2010 Expert

Microsoft Project 2010 Master Class

Microsoft Visio 2010 Essentials

Microsoft Visio 2010 Advanced

Microsoft Visio 2010 Master Class

Coming Soon

Microsoft Access 2013 Essentials

Microsoft Access 2013 Advanced

Microsoft Access 2013 Expert

Microsoft Access 2013 Master Class

Microsoft PowerPoint 2013 Essentials

Microsoft PowerPoint 2013 Advanced

Microsoft PowerPoint 2013 Expert

Microsoft PowerPoint 2013 Master Class

Microsoft Outlook 2013 Essentials

Microsoft Outlook 2013 Advanced

Microsoft Outlook 2013 Expert

Microsoft Outlook 2013 Master Class

Microsoft Publisher 2013 Essentials

Microsoft Publisher 2013 Advanced

Microsoft Publisher 2013 Master Class

Windows 7 Essentials

Windows 8 Essentials

www.ingramcontent.com/pod-product-compliance
Lightning Source LLC
Chambersburg PA
CBHW070836070326
40690CB00009B/1565